ROBERT GORDON'S

THE
1930s

Sally Hewitt

W
FRANKLIN WATTS
LONDON • SYDNEY

I can remember the 1930s

First published in 2005 by Franklin Watts
96 Leonard Street, London EC2A 4XD

Franklin Watts Australia
45-51 Huntley Street
Alexandria, NSW 2015

Series editor: Sarah Peutrill
Series design: White Design
Art director: Jonathan Hair
Design: Matthew Lilly
Picture researcher: Diana Morris

A CIP catalogue record
for this book is available from
the British Library

ISBN 0 7496 5812 6

Printed in Malaysia

Picture credits:
AP/Topham: front cover tl, b, 25c, 29b. Courtesy
of the Cambridge Collection, Cambridge County
Council: 11b. Hulton Deutsch/Corbis: 4b. Kurt
Hutton/Hulton Archive/Getty: 8t.
Picturepoint/Topham: front cover cl, cr, 12t, 13b,
14b, 15t, 15b, 16c, 17t, 17b, 18b, 21b, 22-23b, 24b,
27l, 27r. Popperfoto: 26b, 28t. Sasha/Hulton Archive/Getty: 20b. John
Topham/Topham: 7c. Topham: 9r. Wigan Heritage Services: 19t, 19b.

Every attempt has been made to clear copyright. Should there be any
inadvertent omission please apply to the publisher for rectification.

The author and publisher would like to thank everyone who
contributed their memories and personal photographs to this book.

Contents

Introduction

THE 1930s

In the 1930s, Britain still had a vast empire that included countries all over the world. At home, Britain was recovering from the terrible loss of life as well as the huge cost of World War I (1914–18). People hoped that it had been 'the war to end all wars', but in 1933 Adolf Hitler came to power in Germany and the threat of war hung over Britain once again.

UNEMPLOYMENT

In 1929, the New York Stock Exchange crashed, losing $30,000,000 in one day. Europe was still recovering from World War I and the crash made things worse. By the early 1930s in Britain and elsewhere, industries had become run down, jobs were hard to find and people did not have money to spend. This period was called the Depression.

NEW HOMES AND JOBS

When the Depression began to lift, slums were pulled down and new homes were built. Jobs in the building industry were created and more families could take out a mortgage to buy their own home. New industries such as car manufacturing and electrical engineering began to grow. There were more professional and office jobs than ever before.

← Every year, towns, villages and churches celebrated Empire Day on May 24th. These children are on parade, waving the Union Jack.

NOTE ON 1930s' CURRENCY:

Money came in pounds, shillings and pence – l. s. d. for short. There were 20 shillings to a pound and twelve pence to a shilling. Pennies were divided into halfpennies (pronounced hayp'nies), which were worth half a penny, and farthings, which were worth a quarter of a penny. A crown was five shillings and half a crown was two shillings and six pence.

THEY CAN REMEMBER

In this book eight people share their memories of what it was like to live in Britain in the 1930s. They each have a story to tell in their own section, but they also add other memories throughout the book.

Then

Now

Joyce Clark*

Joyce grew up in a big family in the 1930s. She remembers her mother working hard to make sure there was enough to go round.

*Now Joyce Winspear

Then

Eric Brown

Eric remembers Wigan in the 1930s when the coal mines and cotton mills were still at work. He went to Liverpool University and became a teacher.

Now

Then

Now

Kathleen, Brenda and Peggy Hobbs*

The sisters remember a happy childhood in 1930s' Soham, a village in Cambridgeshire.

* Now Brenda Bott, Peggy Leonard and Kathleen Day

Then

Now

Bill Mellow

Bill left school at 14 and started work in 1930s' London. He joined the navy when he was only 15½.

Then

Val Bamford*

Val remembers seaside holidays during the 1930s at Whitley Bay. She went to a Lyons Corner House for meals with her parents.

*Now Val Abercrombie

Then

Now

Ken Foard

Ken remembers London in the 1930s when streets were still lit by gas lamps and people travelled on trams.

Now

Growing up in a big family

BEDTIME

Joyce was three in 1930, the fifth child in a family of ten children. She doesn't remember a time when she wasn't surrounded by brothers and sisters, sharing food, clothes and their parents' attention. At bedtime, the children shared beds.

Joyce, 1939

> *We had our wash and were put into bed. The eight oldest children slept four to a bed, two at the top, two at the bottom. My mother used to make us say our prayers every single night no matter how tired she was.*

PLAYMATES

Being one of a big family meant there was always someone to play with.

> *We didn't need other people. Other children thought it was wonderful to come round to our house!*

ENOUGH FOR EVERYONE

Joyce's mother worked very hard. She found ways of making what they had go round.

> *My mother sat up every night sewing. She'd buy a dress from the second-hand shop and by the morning, there'd be two dresses.*

NEW SHOES

One day at school, Joyce's teacher humiliated her in front of all her friends for not having a pair of leather shoes.

> *My mother bought me a new pair of plimsolls for best. I was proud of them. The teacher spotted them! She said, 'Right everybody, stand on your forms.' She went round saying, 'Good girl, you shined your shoes this morning.' She got to me and said, 'Your shoes are not shiny.' I said, 'They don't shine, they're plimsolls.' She said, 'Oh what a pity.' You wouldn't be allowed to do that to a child now!*

EMERGENCY

In the 1930s, there was no National Health Service (NHS) to look after you if you were ill. You had to have insurance, pay for treatment or depend on charity. Joyce remembers her brother, Joe, being desperately ill with peritonitis.

> *My mother went off for a whole day carrying him on her shoulders to find a hospital that would take him. We thought he was going to die. After that, everything that was going spare went to Joe. The skin of the custard went to Joe – because he survived.*

← Gravesend Hospital in 1939. Only wage earners were covered by National Insurance in the late 1930s. Local authorities and charities contributed to the cost of treating people without jobs. Most hospitals were run by voluntary organisations and funded by bazaars, flag days and subscriptions.

↓ Joyce's family today, from top left to right: Charles, Joseph (Joe), Joyce, Sylvia, Ada, James, Ruby. Front left to right: Irene, Dorothy, Rose.

STILL TOGETHER

Joyce's family still keep in touch and enjoy family gatherings.

> *It can be quite wearing being in a big family but I wouldn't change it for the world, especially now when we all get together.*

Education

SCHOOLS

In the 1930s, schools were divided into infants, juniors and seniors. Most children left school at 14 and went to work. You could take a scholarship exam for a place at a grammar school and go on to further education.

INFANT SCHOOL

Kathleen remembers the village infant school in Soham.

➡ Slates could be rubbed clean and used again and again.

> 66 *We had slates to write on and cowrie shells to count with. There were rushmats for 'little sleeps' in the afternoon.* 99

Even though the children were young, discipline was strict.

> 66 *One day a boy swore in class. The teacher yanked him out of the classroom and washed his mouth out with carbolic soap. We all just sat there terrified.* 99

NO SCHOOL DINNERS

Bill often had to get through a whole school day with nothing to eat. His school was four and a half miles [seven kilometres] from home.

> 66 *There were no school dinners. If you wanted dinner you ran all the way home and ran back again. Were we fit! We didn't take sandwiches. Half the time there was nothing to make them with!* 99

⬆ Kathleen's class in Soham.

SUNDAY SCHOOL OUTING

Once a year all the Sunday School children got on the train at Soham station, carrying a picnic to be eaten on the beach at Hunstanton, Norfolk. It was always the same – sandwiches, hard-boiled eggs, cream crackers and cheese triangles. Peggy remembers that one year her mum knitted their swimming costumes.

> *They looked so nice with a yacht embroidered on the front, but when we went into the sea, the weight of the water caused them to droop down to our knees!*

CAMPING WITH THE GIRL GUIDES

Brenda looked forward to camping in Hunstanton with the Girl Guides.

> *Mum used to make a big cake for me to take. When I was on cooks' patrol we made porridge you could cut with a knife! We cooked fried cheese dreams. They were lovely.*

SOHAM FEAST SUNDAY

The girls looked forward to Soham Feast Sunday every year. Floats drove through the high street, the Soham band played and there were flower-arranging competitions. Brenda remembers that the bike and running races were a highlight.

> *You used to get sixpence [two and a half pence] for winning a race. With our winnings we bought coconut chips from the sweet stall or a ball on a piece of elastic, and hit everyone on the head with it!*

Kathleen and Peggy still live in Soham and Brenda lives in nearby Newmarket.

⬇ The Soham Comrades Band was formed in 1921, and performed at the Soham Feast Sunday during the 1930s.

11

Childhood

← Children play with their homemade scooters in London's East End.

PLAYING OUTSIDE

In the 1930s there was very little traffic so playing outside was safer than it is today. Bats, balls, hoops, spinning tops and a piece of chalk for hopscotch were all the children needed to have fun.

Ken remembers playing in the London streets.

> *There would be a big group of boys and girls. We put a skipping rope across the road, played with a wooden top and bowled hoops with sticks.*

Joyce's older brothers made trolleys and scooters from old boxes, pieces of wood and wheels.

> *One day I had a ride around the block on my brother's scooter. The thing broke and I put it back in the shed quickly. My brother was going to go round the block with all his mates on his scooter and he said, 'My scooter's broken.' I really had to pay for that!*

PLAYING INSIDE

On winter evenings, Kathleen and her sisters put on shows.

> *We would entertain Mum and Dad with songs and dancing, appearing from behind the door curtain that kept the draught out.*

↑ Hyde Park, London: 15,000 members of The Women's League of Health and Beauty give a display of exercises.

WOMEN'S LEAGUE OF HEALTH AND BEAUTY

Back at home, Val remembers that fitness classes for women were very popular. Val's mother belonged to The Women's League of Health and Beauty.

> *They were all over the country. They wore shiny, satiny, very daring shorts and white silky tops. They all exercised together. It was all rather gentle.*

LYONS CORNER HOUSE

One of Val's favourite treats was to go to a Lyons Corner House.

> *The waitresses were called Nippies. They had little white caps and aprons. There was music, often a ladies' trio. You could have beans on toast or a full meal. It was a great meeting place for people who wanted an inexpensive meal and a bit of atmosphere.*

↑ 'Nippy' waitress Dorothy Porter, 1932.

15

Entertainment

WIRELESS

By the 1930s, many homes had a radio, which was called a wireless set. The BBC was the only radio station in Britain, but you could also tune in to Radio Luxembourg.

CHILDREN'S HOUR

The highlight of Val's day was 'Children's Hour' between five and six p.m., with Uncle Mac. On her sixth birthday, her parents contacted the BBC to give her a special surprise.

> *I had a few friends in for tea. The voice came over the radio. My name was mentioned and I was told to look under the clock in the hall. We all rushed out to the hall and I found a present under the grandfather clock!*

BATTERIES

Many homes did not have electricity, so wireless sets were battery operated. They had an accumulator that had to be recharged about once a week at the local garage. It was Joyce's job to take the accumulator for recharging.

> *My mother always said, 'If you drop that, the whole street will blow up!' I used to walk along very gingerly with it. One day, I was swinging the battery and it dropped. I rushed from house to house banging on doors shouting, 'Get out! Get out! The street's going to blow up!' It didn't …*

SPORT

To watch sport your only option was to go to the matches, otherwise you had to follow the news on the radio or in the newspapers.

! Ken remembers...

"I've always been interested in sport. We followed it on the radio and in the papers. I remember well Perry winning Wimbledon."

⬆ Fred Perry was the last British man to win Wimbledon. He won three years running, in 1934, 1935 and 1936.

! Eric remembers...

"In Wigan there were tennis, cricket and football clubs. There were facilities for tennis and bowls in the well-kept local park."

Cinema

In the 1930s, silent movies gave way to 'talkies', and black and white to colour. Colour films such as *Gone with the Wind* and *The Wizard of Oz* were major successes. Very few homes had television and going to the cinema was very popular. Children queued up to see special film programmes on Saturday mornings. Some of the films were serials – you had to go the next week to see what happened next.

↑ *Gone with the Wind* (1939) cost a record-breaking $4 million to make but eventually made $200 million at the box office.

↑ The abdication of King Edward VIII, December 1936. He abdicated because he wanted to marry Wallace Simpson, a divorcee. As the King he was not allowed to marry a divorcee.

Newsreel

A typical programme at the cinema began with a newsreel followed by a B movie then the main feature film. Everyone stood up for the National Anthem at the end of the programme.

Ken watched the newsreel about the abdication of Edward VIII at the Lewisham Gaumont in London.

" *At the mere appearance of royalty they played 'God Save the King' so we all stood up. Then sat down. Every time they showed another royal person they played 'God Save the King' again. We were up and down like yoyos!* "

Growing up in Wigan

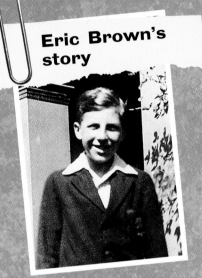

Eric, 1930

COAL AND COTTON

Eric grew up in Wigan in North West England. It was an industrial town built around cotton mills and coal mines surrounded by beautiful countryside.

> *I particularly remember the coalman making his weekly delivery of sacks of coal which he had to carry on his back from his cart to each house. At that time almost all homes were heated by open fires. Their smoking chimneys contributed to the fogs which reduced traffic to a crawl and brought distress to sufferers of chest complaints.*

⬇ Women working at a Lancashire cotton mill. They had to lip-read because of the deafening noise of the looms.

WIGAN PIER

In 1937 George Orwell wrote *The Road to Wigan Pier* about working life in 1930s' Wigan. You can visit Wigan Pier today.

> *Wigan Pier was on a branch of the Leeds to Liverpool Canal, where coal was loaded onto barges to be transported to the port of Liverpool. It is now a heritage site. Close by, one of the large cotton mills has been preserved and the engines which ran the looms are run for visitors.*

Now homes are heated by gas or electricity. All the working mines and cotton mills in Wigan have closed down.

LEISURE TIME

Eric remembers that rugby was a popular local sport.

> 66 *Our football team wasn't doing very well while Wigan at that time was absolutely at the top of the Rugby League.* 99

➡️ Thousands of people queue to see the very popular Wigan Rugby Club in 1935.

BICYCLES

Eric and his friends explored the local area on their bicycles.

> 66 *We made trips to places like Southport or Blackpool or into the country for days out. We'd take sandwiches and a bottle of pop and have a pleasant day out, returning in the evening with the ___ there was a meal wai___ when we got home.*

Wigan Walkin___

• • • • • • • •

"One of the ___ Wigan yea___ Walking D___ processed a___ banners an___ was a gre___ and prou___

➡️ Childre___ banners on___

FAVOURITE FOOD

Eric's mother might have a Lancashire hotpot, tripe and onions or cow's heels ready for him. Sometimes they had fish and chips.

> 66 *Instead of taking away the fish and chips in newspaper, people took it back home in their own basins. There was another delicacy called 'smacks' – slices of potato dipped in batter and fried in the ___* 99

Running the home

HARD WORK

In the 1930s, few married women went out to work but they had plenty to do at home. Many homes had no electricity or running water. Cooking, washing and cleaning had to be done without machines. Running the home was very hard work. In a big family, like Ken's, all the children had to help.

WASH DAY

Families who could afford it paid someone to do their washing. When Ken's father was unemployed, his mother took in washing on Mondays.

> " *Dad used to get up early and light the copper in the scullery and Mum would spend the day washing with the old scrubbing board.* "

> " *Everyone had jobs to do within the house. The kitchen range was operated by a fire. It had an oven and rings on the top and also a little water tank with a brass tap; that had to be black-leaded. The bottom had to be whitened with hearthstone. That was another job that we did.* "

(!) Kathleen remembers...
"*With her scrub brush and Sunlight soap Mum would spend all morning washing, rinsing, boiling and putting the washing through the mangle.*"

Bill's job was to fetch the water.

> " *We used to go down the road for drinking water from the conduit. It had a lion's mouth, a handle on the side to pump the water and a bucket underneath.* "

Dirty washing s scrubbed inst a washboard wooden frame metal ridges – it clean.

Ken remembers...

"I left school at 14, and went to work for my brother Sid as an electrician. He said, 'I'll make you or I'll break you!' He was a hard teacher. One day something went wrong and Sid got really stuck into me – I finished up in tears. I thought, 'I'm not taking this!' So I got on my bike and set out for home. I got a couple of miles when I remembered his words. I thought, 'You're not going to break me!' So I went back and stuck it out."

On one of his bicycle trips, Bill finalised his plan. He would join the Royal Navy.

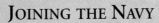

I cycled to Southend for the day with a chum of mine. The British Home Fleet were lying off shore and I saw all these young sailors coming ashore on Southend Pier and I thought, 'Oh yes, that's it! I'll be seeing you!'

JOINING THE NAVY

Bill had to wait until he was 15½ to join up.

One morning, I went to number 85, Whitehall to join the Royal Navy. They gave me a form that your parents had to sign to say you could join. Dad looked at it and he said, 'Are you sure you want to join the Navy?' I said, 'Just sign it, Dad!' And I never regretted it. I'd do it all again."

Into service

Many girls went into service when they left school at 14. This meant doing housework for a family or an institution. Brenda left home and went into service at Newnham College in Cambridge.

"It was something you knew you'd got to do. You couldn't just say, 'I'm not doing this', then run home again. I was homesick and I worked long hours. I had a half-day off every other Sunday. I used to chase down the road to get the bus to Soham and I had to get the eight o'clock bus back – just to see my mum and dad."

The Depression

UNEMPLOYMENT

In 1930, the Depression was taking hold. Over 2,000,000 people were unemployed, bringing hardship to the many families who had no regular wage coming in. Eric remembers the scenes on the streets of Wigan.

> *I remember seeing miners coming back from work still with the grime from the colliery on them. Then, when unemployment came, miners and other factory and manual workers stood at street corners with nothing to do.*

EXTRA MONEY

When Bill's father lost his job, Bill contributed to the family income.

> *I started part-time work when I was 11, delivering groceries. I had to go to the school-board officer. He'd give you a work card and say how many hours you could work. I used to ride a bike or pull a truck three or four miles [6 kilometres], sometimes in the rain or snow.*

⬇ Unemployed men wait by the docks in East London, hoping to pick up a day's work.

❗ Bill remembers...
"Only people who worked on the railways and buses and postmen had permanent jobs."

NEXT MEAL

When Ken's father was out of work, Ken helped his mother with her cleaning jobs.

> *I used to go round and clean walls and scrub paths for which I got 6d. In those days, 6d would feed us. You could go to the butcher and get sausages for 2d. So that money was important. One morning I saw two girls about my age laughing at me scrubbing away. I thought, 'You obviously haven't got to worry about where your next meal's coming from!'*

THE RENT COLLECTOR

In the 1930s most people didn't own their own homes, they rented them. Bill's family often found it hard to scrape enough money together to pay the rent collector when he came round once a week.

> *A lot of people were in the same situation as us at that time. When the rent collector came round my mother said, 'Be quiet, don't make a noise!' In other words, we were out!*

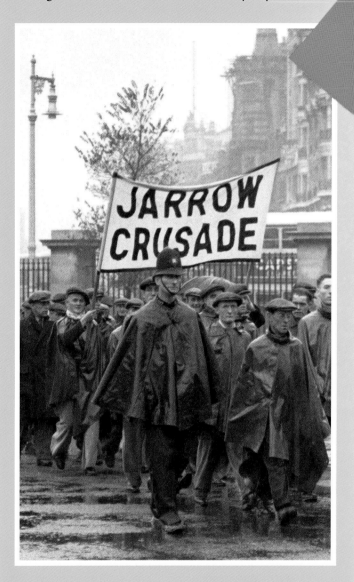

⬇ A policeman escorts the Jarrow marchers through the streets of London on a rainy day.

Jarrow march

●●●●●●●●●●●●●●●●●●●●●●●●●●●●●●●●●●

In 1936, 200 unemployed shipyard workers began a long protest march from Jarrow, a town in north-east England, to London. They were taking a petition to Westminster to protest against the loss of jobs in the shipyards and the iron and steel industry. The march took 26 days, but Prime Minister Stanley Baldwin refused to meet them to accept their petition.

London between the wars

LEGACY OF WAR

World War I (1914–18) was meant to be 'the war to end all wars' but only 21 years later, in 1939, World War II broke out.

Ken's father fought in World War I during which his health was damaged.

> *Dad was badly gassed during World War I but in those days there was no pension for those sorts of things. His lungs were eaten away.*

Ken Foard's story

Ken, 1939

MOVING

After World War I, the munitions factory at Woolwich in London was closed down. For a cheap rent Ken's family moved into an estate of wooden huts originally built for factory workers.

> *Occasionally the huts did catch fire and they were burnt to the ground. But there were very few incidents and people were careful.*

DOLE MONEY

During the Depression, Ken's father was unemployed for two years.

> *He had to walk three miles [nearly five kilometres] each way to Woolwich to sign on. He had to sign on twice a week and then the third time he drew the dole money he was entitled to.*

← Men sitting reading newspapers in an unemployment club, 1936.

TALES AND TALK

Ken and his friends used to look out for the lamp lighter and the night watchman. They were always ready to chat and tell the boys a good tale.

Lamp lighter

" *The streets were lit with gas lamps. The lamp lighter came round on a push-bike just before dusk and again at dawn. The lamps all had a pilot light. He switched the gas on and off. He was a friendly type.* "

← Each gas lamp in the streets of London had to be lit by hand at dusk and extinguished the next morning at dawn.

Night watchman

" *When there were road works, the night watchman lit hurricane lamps and put them round the road works. He had a brazier filled with hot coals or wood. We would sit round and join him and he would tell us stories about his life and his past.* "

TRAMS

During the 1930s electric trams running on tracks carried passengers along the London streets. Ken and his friends used the trams to help them find their way through the thickest of London smogs.

↑ London trams were a reliable form of transport. They were never held up by traffic jams.

" *In those days we had smogs. They were yellow. You couldn't see your hand in front of you. When we were cycling we'd get between the lines and follow the tram so you didn't have to worry. The old trams never let you down.* "

SWIMMING POOL

The boys used to swim in the local pool but there was no mixed bathing.

" *You had days for boys and days for girls. As time went on there was one day a week for mixed bathing.* "

Threat of war

HITLER COMES TO POWER

Fathers who fought in World War I (1914–18) never thought they would see their sons fight in another world war. But when Hitler came to power in Germany in 1933, the threat of war grew stronger each year.

CHURCH PARADE

Ken's father had been a gunner in World War I. During the 1930s he used to take Ken to watch the church parade at the barracks in Woolwich.

> " *On the parade ground you'd see cadets from all over the world. Some of the Japanese officers we ended up fighting were trained at Woolwich!* "

⬆ So many young recruits joined up and began their training that, in 1939, uniforms were not always ready for them.

FIGHTING FOR YOUR COUNTRY

By the time Ken left school and went to work, he was aware that war was looming. Young men of his age knew they would be called on to fight for their country. Ken joined the Signals where he could use his skills as an electrician.

> " *I'm very much a flag waver [a patriot]. The country was being threatened! I queued for nearly three hours because of all the people wanting to join up. Would you see that today? I don't know. I like to think that they would turn out for the old country.* "

Bill had already joined the Navy. When he finished his training he went to sea.

> 66 *In the September of 1938 we were close to war. We went full speed from the Greek islands to Alexandria [in Egypt] to join the rest of the fleet. All the ammunition in the ship was fused ready for firing if needed. Then the panic died down.* 99

END OF CAREFREE CHILDHOOD
The threat of war affected children in many different ways:
● Seaside holidays: coils of barbed wire cut off beaches to stop enemy invasion.
● Guide camps: the war stopped Peggy and Kathleen going on Guide camps as their sister had.

● Evacuation: children were separated from their parents to be sent to safer places, usually in the countryside. Joyce's mother told her they had to be evacuated.

> 66 *I thought you could pick up a bomb and throw it back again. I had no idea. But she said, 'If you stay here we could get bombed and we'll all die.' I said, 'Okay, so we'll all die together!'* 99

Joyce and her brothers and sisters were all evacuated to Kent.

WAR IS DECLARED
In 1939, Hitler marched into Poland. Britain and France challenged him to withdraw. He refused and on 3rd September, Britain and France declared war against Germany.

⬆ Hitler being greeted by enthusiastic crowds on the streets of Saarbrüken, in western Germany, in October 1938.

Timeline

1930

May Amy Johnson becomes the first woman to fly alone from Britain to Australia.
August Unemployment reaches over two million in Britain.

1931

14th April The King of Spain abdicates and flees to London.

1932

8th November Franklin D. Roosevelt is elected President of the USA. He promises Americans 'A New Deal'.

1933

30th January Adolf Hitler becomes Chancellor of Germany.
23rd October A new Lyons Corner House opens in London. It can cater for 2,000 people at a time.

1934

April The government announces a boom in house building.
7th July Englishman Fred Perry wins the tennis championship at Wimbledon – the first of three victories in a row.

1935

April Dust storms sweep through the 'bread basket' states of America.
6th May The Silver Jubilee of King George V.

1936

January King George V dies.
July A new board game called 'Monopoly' arrives in the shops.

October 200 unemployed men march in protest from Jarrow to London.
December King Edward VIII abdicates and hands the throne to his younger brother.

1937

March *The Road to Wigan Pier* by George Orwell is published.
May 12th Coronation of George VI.
May 28th Neville Chamberlain becomes prime m̶i̶n̶i̶s̶t̶e̶r̶

1938

March ▉
29th Se ▉
German ▉
30th Se ▉
Neville ▉
our tim ▉
1st Oct ▉
Sudeten ▉

1939

15th M ▉
Prague, ▉
prepares ▉
1st Sept ▉
Poland. ▉
3rd Septe ▉
war again ▉

Glossary

Abdication To abdicate means to give up something. When Edward VIII abdicated, he gave up the throne to his younger brother. This was called the 'Abdication'.

Black lead A black powder rubbed into fire grates and stoves to make them black and shiny.

B movie A movie shown before the main feature film at the cinema.

Brazier A metal basket for hot coals. Night-watchmen sat round a brazier to keep warm.

Cadet A trainee in the armed services.

Copper A big copper container for boiling water used for doing the laundry.

Cowrie shells Small sea shells used by school children to help them learn to count.

Diphtheria An infectious disease which affects the throat making it difficult and painful to swallow.

Grant Money given to students to help them with their studies.

Gunner A soldier in the artillery (large guns) division of the British army.

Hearthstone A soft stone that was rubbed over a wet hearth or doorstep to whiten them.

Hurricane lamp An oil lamp with a transparent case to protect the flame from the wind.

Mangle Two rollers turned with a handle used to squeeze water out of wet washing.

Newsreel A reel of film showing news stories at the cinema before the B movie and the feature film.

Patriot Someone who is proud of their country.

Peritonitis A serious inflammation of the lining of the abdomen that needs immediate surgery.

Plimsolls Canvas gym shoes with rubber soles.

Scarlet fever An infectious fever bringing a sore throat, sickness and a red-coloured rash.

Scullery A small room next to the kitchen for cleaning cutlery or peeling vegetables.

Smallholding A small farm with a few animals and a vegetable garden.

Smog A thick yellow fog caused by smoke from factory chimneys and household fires.

Tripe Part of a cow's stomach. It can be cooked in stews and casseroles.

Tuberculosis An infection of the lungs.

Index